Standard Chord Symbol Notation

(A Uniform System for the Music Profession)

by
Carl Brandt
and
Clinton Roemer

© Clinton H. Roemer 1976

Sole Selling Agent:
Roerick Music Co.
4046 Davana Road
Sherman Oaks, Calif. 91423

All rights reserved. No part of this book may be reproduced in any form, or by any means, without permission in writing from the publisher.

Printed in the United States of America

ISBN 0-9612684-2-5

Table of Contents

Preface 5
Chapter 1. Toward a Uniform System 7
     2. The Raw Material of Chords 9
     3. Basic Rules 11
         Graphics 12
     4. Major Chords 13
         Major Triads 13
         Major Triads With Added Sixth 13
         Major Triads With Added Sixth & Ninth 14
         Major Triads With Added Ninth Only 14
         Dominant Sevenths 15
         Dominant Ninths 15
         Dominant Elevenths 16
         Dominant Thirteenths 17
         Major Sevenths 18
         Major Ninths 18
     5. Minor Chords 19
         Minor Triads 19
         Minor Triads With Added Sixth 19
         Minor Triads With Added Sixth & Ninth 20
         Minor Triads With Added Ninth Only 20
         Minor Sevenths 20
         Minor Ninths 21
         Minor Elevenths 21
         Minor Thirteenths 22
         Minor Triads With Major Seventh 23
         Minor Ninths With a Major Seventh 23
     6. Diminished Chords 24
         Diminished Sevenths 24
         Diminished Triads 24
     7. Augmented Chords 25
         Augmented Triads 25
         Augmented (Dominant) Sevenths & Ninths 25
         Augmented Major Sevenths & Ninths 25
         Augmented Minor Triads & Minor Sevenths . . . 26
     8. Suspensions 27
         Suspended Diminished Sevenths 28
     9. Chords With Altered Functions 29
         Flat Fifths 29
         Altered Ninths 31
         Altered Fifths & Ninths Combined 32
         Altered Elevenths 34
    10. Compound Chords 36
    11. Polytonal Chords 39
    12. Miscellany 41
         Fourth Chords 41
         Omitted Notes 41
         Concerning Registers 42
    13. In Summation 44
About the Authors 45

Preface

Much unnecessary confusion exists today in the notation, interpretation and graphic representation of chord symbols in music. Like its predecessor, the figured bass, the chord symbol is nothing more than a form of musical shorthand intended to convey to the performer as much information as possible, in as short a time as possible, with the greatest lucidity possible. Unfortunately, these objectives have almost been overlooked in the attempt by the composer/arranger to give too much detail, thereby cluttering up the symbol with unwieldy appendages, or to give too little detail, hence denying the player the data he needs to make the best musical sense.

It can be argued that the creation of music is a constantly evolving process and that its increasing complexities demand more intricate methods of notation. In the milieu of contemporary pop-rock-jazz-commercial-music-for-the-esoteric-common-folk, so many harmonic innovations have become a part of the fabric that top-heavy arrays of numerals, pluses, minuses and verbal instructions are considered *de rigueur*. This need not be. To be sure, there will be occasions when the shorthand of chord symbols is an insufficiency; in this event the chord should be written out in notation instead of creating some sort of time-wasting, undecipherable musical acrostic that will serve only to muddy the sound at that moment.

The welter of disparate chord symbol expressions abounding today quite possibly were contrived by the self-taught to display a new musical sophistication. On second thought, they would seem instead to have sprung from expediency, lack of practical experience, or, most likely, insufficient technique in harmonic analysis. Regrettably, some of these aberrations can also be laid at the doorsteps of those who teach jazz courses in the schools.

It is beyond the scope of this volume to include a treatise on harmony, but it should be said that an understanding of harmonic fundamentals is vital to writing easily understandable chord symbols and comprehending the logic of their structures.

Acceptance of and adherence to a set of ground rules containing no ambiguities or exotica provides a firm footing for composer, arranger, music copyist and player alike. The standardization of the language of chord symbols and their proper physical placement on the page will contribute greatly to easier reading, a quicker grasp of the composer/arranger's meaning and, above all, a better performance.

THE AUTHORS

All examples shown in the text as "UNACCEPTABLE" have been taken from the scores of professional composer/arrangers, work by copyists, writings by music educators, and from published music.

The pitch-name of any chord shown herein is purely an arbitrary choice. It is to be understood that the text refers to chords of all pitches.

Chapter 1

Toward a Uniform System

As things stand today, a musician dealing with chord symbols is working at a definite disadvantage. Confronted as he is with a bewildering array of non-related hieroglyphs presented in a variety of graphic forms, it is fortunate that as much intelligence is communicated as does get set forth.

The fault lies in the lack of standardization and uniformity of chord symbols, and can be traced to the professional as well as the novice, not to overlook the enterprising amateur who may have devised his own innovations.

When changing the unsuitable (to him) form of a chord symbol, the arranger or copyist has been known to bring into play his own cabalistic system of further abbreviations, obfuscating the issue that much more.

It must be kept in mind that chord symbols comprise a musical language, and that language, especially for the instrumentalist who is reading it for the first time, must be kept as succinct and free from variants as possible.

This can be best illustrated by showing a group of variants for only 4 common chords:

[F_{MA}^7] MAJOR SEVENTH

F^7	$F^\triangle$	$F^{\triangle 7}$	$F^{\natural 7}$	$F^{7\natural}$	$F(\sharp 7)$
$F7\sharp$	$F(7\sharp)$	F^{7+}	$F(+7)$	$F_M{}^7$	FM^7
$FM7$	F_{MA}	$F_{MAJ}{}^7$	$F_{ma}{}^7$	$F_{mj}{}^7$	$F_{ma}{}^7$
$F_{maj}{}^7$	F_{MA}^7	$FMaj^7$	FMJ^7	F_{MA}^7	F_M^7

[F^7] DOMINANT (SMALL) SEVENTH

F^7	$F\,7th$	$F^{\natural 7}$	$F^{7\natural}$	$F(\flat 7)$	$F^{7\flat}$	$F(7\flat)$
F_7	$F(E\flat)$	$F(ADD\,E\flat)$	$F_{ADD}{}^7$	F^{7-}	$F(-7)$	$F(+7)$

[Fmi^7] MINOR SEVENTH

Fmi^7	Fm^7	$Fmin^7$	$Fmin^7$	$F\underline{m}^7$	Fm^7	$Fmi^{(7)}$
$Fm(Eb)$	$F7(b3)$	$F-7$	$F7(Ab)$	$FMIN7$	$Fmi^{\underline{7}}$	F^7min
FMi^7	$Fmi7$	F^7mi	Fmi^7	F^7m	F^{m7}	$Fmi7$

[$Fmi^{7(b5)}$] MINOR SEVENTH WITH A FLAT FIFTH

Fmi^75-	$F\triangle$	$F\triangle 7$	Fm^{7-5}	$Fmin^{7(5b)}$	$Fmi^{7(Cb)}$	$F\emptyset 7$
$F\phi$	$FMIN^{7-5}$	$Fmi^{7(5-)}$	$Fmi^7 5^b$	$F-7-5$	$F-7(-5)$	$F-7(5b)$
$Fmi7^{(5-)}$	$F\underline{7}_m-5$	F^7mi5-	$F7(b3\,b5)$	$F\underline{m}^7(5b)$	$F^{(-5)}_{Mi7}$	$B6(b5)$

The dilemma reveals itself with only a cursory inspection of the foregoing examples.

Commonly, almost all notators of music are certain that their own system of symbol writing is superior to others, but an examination of their efforts often uncovers many inconsistencies.

The following excerpt from a score by an eminent professional arranger is typical and will serve to illustrate:

$$D^b MAJ^7 \quad D^{b7}_m \quad D^{b7}$$

Here, while an elaborate symbol for the MAJOR 7TH CHORD is employed, the requisite information for the MINOR 7TH CHORD is obscured. The symbol for the DOMINANT 7TH CHORD is correct.

Uniformity in writing is indispensable.

Chapter 2

The Raw Material of Chords

Fundamentally and traditionally, the formation of chord structures is accomplished by piling up intervals of the third, one on top of the other, until the desired harmony is achieved. Further intensities are reached by the chromatic alteration of these building blocks, whose given names never change, even though modified chromatically. Any other approach is fallacious.

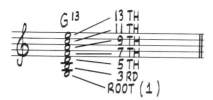

Ever-changing harmonic concepts have dimmed the strict relationship of the DOMINANT SEVENTH (or NINTH) CHORD to the tonic (home-base) tonality, and a chord structure today is its own entity without necessarily having any arbitrary sense of direction. Nevertheless, we must go back to the old dominant-tonic relationship to define a SEVENTH CHORD, abiding by the following rules:

1. The interval of the seventh is always a <u>small</u> 7th unless altered:

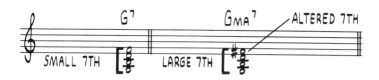

2. In chords having higher functions (9ths, 11ths, 13ths), the small seventh is assumed to be present, unless altered:

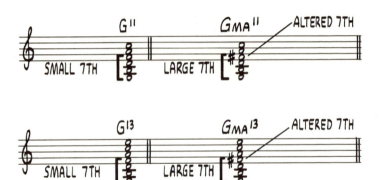

3. In general, a suspension relates to the 3rd of the chord. Here, the 4th degree of the scale replaces the 3rd and is the suspension:

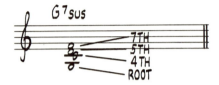

4. The term "sixth" (6th) is used only with major or minor triads in the sense of "added 6th". It is never used with DOMINANT 7TH, 9TH, 11TH or 13TH CHORDS.

5. The root of the chord must always be given, and any inversion indicated. Special cases and COMPOUND CHORDS will be discussed later.

The basic premise, then, is that chords are built on 3rds, and not on scales.

Chapter 3
Basic Rules

To achieve a uniform and standard system of chord symbols, the following basic rules are presented:

1. Use only CAPITAL LETTERS for chord names:

   C D E F G A B

2. Use only NECESSARY words and abbreviations, written only in UPPER CASE letters approximately one-half the size of those used for chord names, as follows:

   MA MI SUS ADD OMIT PURE

   MA   Signifies MAJOR. Used only when followed by numeral "7", "9", "11" or "13" to indicate the presence of the interval of the MAJOR SEVENTH.

   MI   Signifies MINOR.

   SUS   Signifies SUSPENSION.

   ADD   Indicates the addition of a single note to a chord, as in "C (ADD 9)".

   OMIT   Indicates omission of a single note from a chord, as in "C (OMIT 3)".

   PURE   Signifies the indicated chord is to be used in its basic form, with no discretionary added notes.

3. Use the PLUS SIGN (+) ONLY to indicate the AUGMENTED FIFTH.

4. Use the SMALL CIRCLE (o) ONLY to indicate the DIMINISHED SEVENTH CHORD.

5. Use the SHARP (♯) ONLY to indicate a **raised** function, such as a SHARP NINTH (♯9).

6. Use the FLAT (♭) ONLY to indicate a lowered function, such as a FLAT FIFTH (♭5).

7. In altered functions, the SHARP or FLAT always PRECEDES the numeral: (♭5, not 5♭; ♯9, not 9♯).

8. Use PARENTHESES ( ) to enclose any and all changes in the basic chord, such as (♯9), (♭5), (OMIT 3), (ADD 9), (PURE), and so on. A SUSPENSION is not considered to be an altered function, and its abbreviation, SUS, is not parenthesized.

9. *DO NOT USE THE FOLLOWING SYMBOLS; ELIMINATE THEM COMPLETELY:*

   MINUS SIGN (–)   The worst offender of all. It has been used to signify a MINOR CHORD, a DIMINISHED SEVENTH CHORD, and to act as a substitute for the FLAT, such as (–5) and (5–).

TRIANGLE (△)   The Greek letter DELTA currently has two interpretations: MAJOR SEVENTH and MINOR SEVENTH WITH A FLAT FIFTH, the so-called HALF-DIMINISHED CHORD.

THETA (⊖)   In use to indicate the HALF-DIMINISHED CHORD.

PHI (ɸ and ∅)   Also in use to indicate the HALF-DIMINISHED CHORD.

EUROPEAN SEVEN (7̶)   Adopted by a number of Americans to signify the MAJOR SEVENTH chord. In the European context it means the DOMINANT SEVENTH, the chord containing the small 7th, not the MAJOR (large) 7th. The cross bar on the numeral seven is used by Europeans to distinguish it from their numeral one. Music being an international language, the American symbol (CMA7) is perfectly understood overseas, while the European numeral seven is ambiguous.

1 = European numeral one.
7̶ = European numeral seven.

AUG   Replace the abbreviation for AUGMENTED by the PLUS SIGN (+) to indicate the AUGMENTED FIFTH. (To repeat, this is the only valid use of the PLUS SIGN. It is not used to indicate a SHARP, such as ("+9" for "♯9".)

---——————————Graphics———————————---

For the sake of clarity and to eliminate the disorder caused by careless writing, a uniform and standardized system of chord symbol graphics is used throughout this book. These forms should be universally adopted.

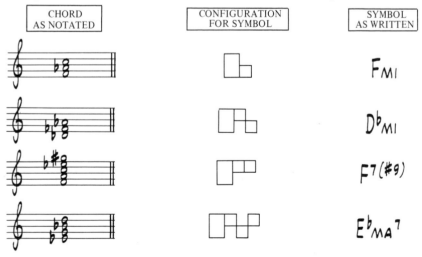

Chapter 4
Major Chords

Major Triads

[musical notation: F, E♭ triads]

CONFIGURATIONS: ☐ F G A B   ⌐ E♭ C♯ A♭

Use only the capital letter (and accidental, when needed).

UNACCEPTABLE:

C$_{MA}$ E♭$_{MAJ}$ F$_{ma}$ G♭$_{maj}$ E$_{mj}$ d e f b g

The addition of "MA" is often used by some writers with the intention of emphasizing "MAJOR", but is also used by others to mean that the MAJOR 7TH is to be added by the player. Avoid confusion by using "MA" only with MAJOR 7TH and MAJOR 9TH CHORDS, as in CMA7 and CMA9.

(CMI / CMA /) — Used by some to indicate change of E-flat to E-natural. Eliminate MA to avoid the unwanted MAJOR 7TH. (CMI / C /) is sufficient and correct.

(E♭ / E♮ /) — Eliminate the natural cancelling the flat; it is not needed.

Major Triads with Added Sixth

[musical notation: C6, F♯6]

CONFIGURATIONS: ⌐ C6 F6   ⌐ F♯6 E♭6

UNACCEPTABLE:

C$_{MA}$6 D♭$_{MAJ}$6 F$\underline{6TH}$ E♭(ADD C)
F(D) C$_6$ F♯$_6$ G♭$_6$ A♭6

(The addition of "MA" or "MAJ" is redundant.)

Major Triads with Added Sixth & Ninth

(The 6/9 CHORD is not to be confused with the 13TH CHORD, which includes the small 7th as well as the 6th and 9th.)

CONFIGURATIONS: ▱ C6/9   ▱ Eb6/9   F#6/9

UNACCEPTABLE: G6(ADD 9) F6(ADD G) C13(OMIT 7) D69
F#13(NO 7) Db6/9 Gb6/9 A2/6 Bb6(2)

C9(NO 7)   This is used erroneously in naming the 6/9 CHORD. Note that no reference is made to the added 6th.

Major Triads with Added Ninth Only

CONFIGURATIONS: ▯ C(ADD 9)   ▯ Ab(ADD 9)

UNACCEPTABLE: C(9) D(ADD 2) E(+9) F(+G) F#2
G9(OMIT 7) A9(NO 7) Bb(ADD C)

Dominant Sevenths

Stemming from traditional harmony, "DOMINANT" is used here to indicate that the 7th of the chord is a small 7th distant from the root. The term "MINOR 7TH" is omitted to avoid confusion with the entity of the complete MINOR 7TH CHORD, which is discussed in Chapter 5.

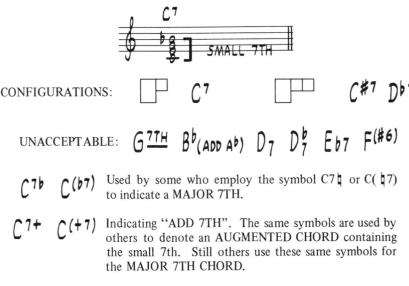

CONFIGURATIONS: ⌐ C^7 ⌐ $C^{\#7}$ $D^{\flat 7}$

UNACCEPTABLE: $G\underline{^{7TH}}$ $B^\flat(\text{ADD } A^\flat)$ D_7 $D^\flat_7$ $E^\flat 7$ $F^{(\#6)}$

$C^{7\flat}$ $C^{(\flat 7)}$ Used by some who employ the symbol $C7\natural$ or $C(\natural 7)$ to indicate a MAJOR 7TH.

C^{7+} $C^{(+7)}$ Indicating "ADD 7TH". The same symbols are used by others to denote an AUGMENTED CHORD containing the small 7th. Still others use these same symbols for the MAJOR 7TH CHORD.

For additional UNACCEPTABLE symbols see page 7.

Dominant Ninths

(Again, "DOMINANT" is used to indicate the small 7th. In any so-called DOMINANT 9TH, accepted practice dictates that the small 7th be present.)

CONFIGURATIONS: ⌐ C^9 ⌐ $B^{\flat 9}$ $F^{\#9}$

UNACCEPTABLE: C^9_7 $C^{\#7}(\text{ADD } D\#)$ $F7(\text{ADD } 9)$ $G^{7(+A)}$ A^7_2

   Used mistakenly to indicate "ADD 9TH". The same symbol is also in use by some to indicate a SHARP 9TH.

Dominant Elevenths

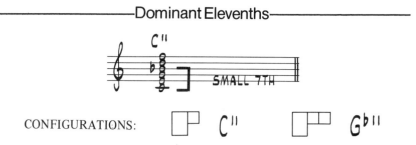

The eleventh is merely one more third placed above the ninth; the term "DOMINANT" again indicates the presence of the small 7th. In general, the third of the ELEVENTH CHORD is omitted to avoid the dissonant interval of the minor ninth between the third and the eleventh, especially when the chord is in the close position:

UNACCEPTABLE:

$D^{9(11)}$ $E^{b9(ADD\ Ab)}$ $C^{9(+11)}$ G^{b}_{11} F^{11}_{9} $A^{b7}(^{11}_{9})$

$C^{9}sus$ The 3rd is not in this chord, being suspended.

A different symbol can be used to ensure that the 3rd of the ELEVENTH CHORD is not played. In this case, it is called "G MINOR 7TH WITH A C BASS". The symbol to the left of the slash bar is the upper structure, a chord, while the capital letter following the slash bar names the bass tone, a <u>single note</u> only:

(The symbol above is called a "COMPOUND CHORD". It is discussed further in Chapter 10.)

If the complete ELEVENTH CHORD of all six notes is wanted, a "POLY-TONAL" symbol can be used. In this case it is called "B-FLAT OVER C", consisting of two major triads on top of each other. This ensures that all 6 notes (including the 3rd) will be present. The bar separating the two components is <u>horizontal</u>.

(This symbol is treated in more detail in Chapter 11 under "POLYTONAL CHORDS".)

Dominant Thirteenths

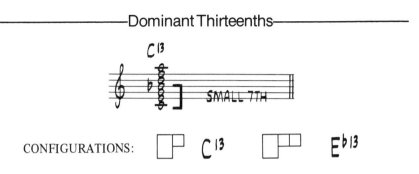

Adding a third to the ELEVENTH CHORD produces the THIRTEENTH CHORD. Once again, "DOMINANT" implies the inclusion of the small 7th.

The example above shows the complete 13TH CHORD with all 7 notes.

In accepted usage, the 9th is included but the 11th is omitted. Quite frequently the unaltered 5th is also left out.

As in the case of the ELEVENTH CHORD, a POLYTONAL symbol may be substituted for the full THIRTEENTH CHORD, in this instance:

The **THIRTEENTH CHORD** is often confused with and referred to mistakenly as a 6/9 CHORD. By definition, the 6/9 CHORD does not contain the small 7th with its "dominant" feeling, and suggests no movement.

Ergo, although the 6th and the 13th have the same tonality, they are two different functions and not interchangeable. In the close position, the 6th lies next to the 5th, whereas the 13th's place is where its name implies: an interval of a 13th distant from the root of the chord.

UNACCEPTABLE:

D7(ADD B)   C7(+A)   E♭7(+6)   F7(ADD 6)   G7(E)
E♭9(ADD C) A9(+F#) G♭9(6)   C9(A)   E9(ADD 6TH)

──────────────── Major Sevenths ────────────────

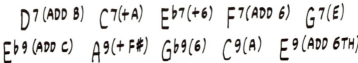

CONFIGURATIONS: ⌐┘ Cma⁷   ⌐┐┘ F#ma⁷

UNACCEPTABLE:

C7   B♭△   C#(#7)   D7#   E♭(+7)   F7+   G♭(♮7)   A7♮   B⑦

For additional UNACCEPTABLE symbols see page 7.

──────────────── Major Ninths ────────────────

CONFIGURATIONS: ⌐┘ Cma⁹   ⌐┐┘ E♭ma⁹

In the case of the MAJOR 9TH CHORD, is it implicit that the major (large) 7th is present in the structure. This is common practice and universally accepted for the sake of brevity.

UNACCEPTABLE:

C7(9)   C#9(7)   Dma7(9)   D♭⁹maj   E♭7(+9)   F⁹⁄₇   G⁹   A9(MA 7)

Chapter 5

Minor Chords

―――――――――――――― Minor Triads ――――――――――――――

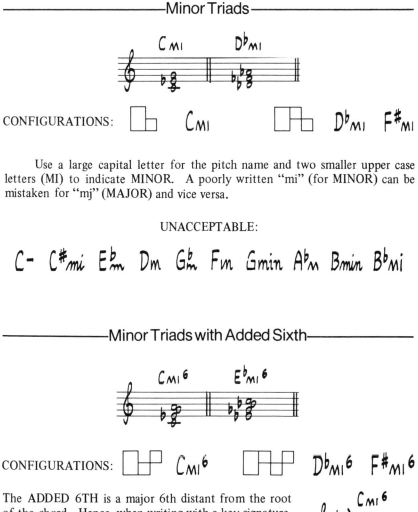

Use a large capital letter for the pitch name and two smaller upper case letters (MI) to indicate MINOR. A poorly written "mi" (for MINOR) can be mistaken for "mj" (MAJOR) and vice versa.

UNACCEPTABLE:

C-   C#mi   E♭m   Dm   G♭m   Fm   Gmin   A♭m   Bmin   B♭mi

―――――――――――― Minor Triads with Added Sixth ――――――――――――

CONFIGURATIONS:

The ADDED 6TH is a major 6th distant from the root of the chord. Hence, when writing with a key signature, the 6th must be raised one-half step. In common use this is tacitly understood (in the context of the ascending melodic minor scale), and the alteration is not indicated in the chord symbol:

UNACCEPTABLE:

C-6   C#m(ADD A#)   Dmi+6   E♭m6   F6m   F#MI(D#)   Gmi(♮6)

Minor Triads with Added Sixth & Ninth

C_{MI} 6/9

CONFIGURATIONS: C_{MI} 6/9 E^b_{MI} 6/9 $C^{\#}_{MI}$ 6/9

(Do not associate this chord with the MINOR 13TH. The 6/9 CHORD does not contain the 7th.)

UNACCEPTABLE: $C^{-6/9}$ $C^{\#-6/9}$ $D_{MI}{}^6{}_{ADD}{}^9$ $D^b{}_{mi}{}^{6(+E^b)}$ $F^{6}_{m}{}^{+9}$
$C^{13\,(OMIT\,7)}_{m}$ $G_{m13}{}^{(NO\,7)}$ $C^{\#}\underline{m6}/9$ $E_m{}^{13}$ $F_m{}^{6}_{9}$

Minor Triads with Added Ninth Only

$C_{MI}{}^{(ADD\,9)}$

CONFIGURATIONS: $C_{MI}{}^{(ADD\,9)}$ $D^b{}_{MI}{}^{(ADD\,9)}$

UNACCEPTABLE:

$C_m{}^{(+9)}$ $D^{b-(+9)}$ $E_{mi}{}^{(9+)}$ $F_{min}{}^{(G)}$ $G_{MI}{}^{(+A)}$ $A_{mi}{}^2$ $B_{mi}{}^{9(NO\,7)}$

Minor Sevenths

$C_{MI}{}^7$

SMALL 7TH

CONFIGURATIONS: $C_{MI}{}^7$ $E^b{}_{MI}{}^7$ $F^{\#}_{MI}{}^7$

UNACCEPTABLE:

C^{-7} D^{-7} $D^{b\bar{7}}$ $E_m{}^7$ $F_m{}^7$ $F^{\#\,7}_{m}$ $G_{mi}{}^{\bar{7}}$ A_{min7} $B^{b7}{}_{MI}$

For additional UNACCEPTABLE symbols see page 8.

Minor Ninths

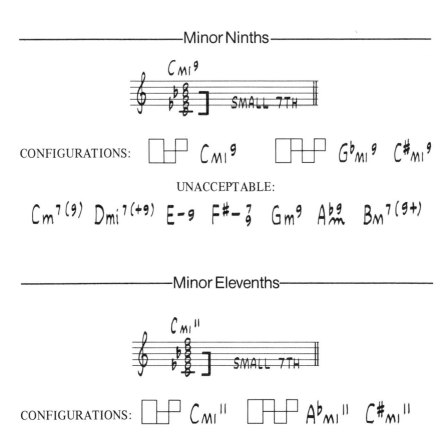

(Particular care should be taken in writing this symbol, there being so many vertical elements involved.)

Generally, no notes are omitted from the MINOR 11TH CHORD, instrumentation permitting. A POLYTONAL symbol (see page 39) may be used to express the full MINOR ELEVENTH CHORD. In this case it is:

The POLYTONAL symbol states unmistakably that 6 notes are to be played.

UNACCEPTABLE:

$C{-}11 \quad D^{b\,11}_{mi} \quad E^{11}_{M} \quad F^{M11} \quad F\#{-}7(^{11}_{9}) \quad Gmi^{7}(^{9}_{11}) \quad A_{MIN}\,11$

Minor Thirteenths

CONFIGURATIONS: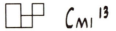

Again, when writing in a key signature, the 13th must be raised one-half step. (See page 19, MINOR TRIADS WITH ADDED 6TH.)

The 13th and the 6th are two separate functions and not interchangeable. Each occupies a different position in the chord.

The 11th is usually omitted from the MINOR 13TH CHORD, so it is felt that the symbol "CMI 13" is sufficient except when all seven notes must be identified.

As in the case of the MINOR 11TH CHORD, a POLYTONAL symbol may be substituted for the full MINOR THIRTEENTH CHORD, in this instance:

UNACCEPTABLE:

$Cmi^{9(13)}$ $D^{b}mi^{7(13)}$ Dm^{6}_{9} $E^{b}_{m}{}^{9\,(ADD\,C)}$ F^{13}_{m}

$F\#^{-9(+13)}$ $G_{MIN}{}^{9(+6)}$ $A^{b\,9}_{min}{}^{(ADD\,6)}$ $B^{b}_{m}{}^{9(\natural 6)}$

Minor Triads with a Major Seventh

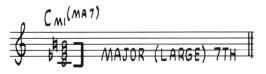

CONFIGURATIONS:

Often the symbol "Eb+" or "Eb AUG" is used incorrectly to mean C MINOR WITH A MAJOR 7TH. Eb+ alone ignores the root of the chord, "C", and does not give all the information needed.

Again, do not use the EUROPEAN 7 to signify a MAJOR 7TH CHORD. (Refer to the explanation given on page 12.)

UNACCEPTABLE:

C-maj7   D-7̸   Emi7̸   F7̸m   Gmin(ma7)   Am7̸   B♭m mj7

Minor Ninths with a Major Seventh

Here, the word "MINOR" refers, obviously, to the basic triad, not the 9th.

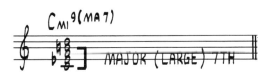

CONFIGURATIONS:

UNACCEPTABLE:

C-9(♯7)   Dm9mj7   D♭-9(7̸)   Emi9̸

F9̸m+7   Gmin7(9)   A♭9m(7+)   B♭mi9(7♯)

Chapter 6
Diminished Chords

―――――――――――Diminished Sevenths―――――――――――

D°   D#°   E°

CONFIGURATIONS: ▟▀ D°   ▟▀ D#° Eb°

A small circle ("o") is the only symbol used to identify the complete DIMINISHED 7TH CHORD. The 7th is tacitly assumed to be included. Hence the numeral "7" is omitted from the symbol. DIMINISHED TRIADS without the 7th are discussed at the bottom of this page.

Sonically, there are only three DIMINISHED 7TH CHORDS, regardless of their inversion. Except in the strict academic sense, the notation of the DIMINISHED 7TH has grown to be a matter of convenience, and in common practice much use is made of enharmonic substitutions. The rationalization for this might be that the DIMINISHED 7TH, being composed of three minor thirds stacked on top of each other, merely repeats itself vertically into infinity and sounds the same (except for register) no matter how it is spelled. Attention must be paid to its root, or bass note, however. For example, when the expression "D DIMINISHED" is used for a pure DIMINISHED 7TH CHORD, a D must be in the bass, not an F (E-sharp), or A-flat (G-sharp), or C-flat (B-natural). The bass note indicates the structure's inversion.

UNACCEPTABLE:

D−   Eb dim   F(DIM)   F#°7   G−7   A7 DIM   Bb7°

(The SUSPENDED DIMINISHED SEVENTH is discussed in Chapter 8, page 28.)

―――――――――――Diminished Triads―――――――――――

A DIMINISHED CHORD is understood to be a 4-part structure, containing the 7th. The DIMINISHED TRIAD (3 parts) omits the 7th and is best described as a MINOR TRIAD WITH A FLAT FIFTH; no written reference to DIMINISHED is made.

Dmi(b5)

CONFIGURATIONS: ▟▀ Dmi(b5)   ▟▀ Ebmi(b5)

UNACCEPTABLE:

D−   E°   Fdim   Gdim   A°(TRIAD)   Bb°(NO 7)   B°(OMIT 7)

Chapter 7
Augmented Chords

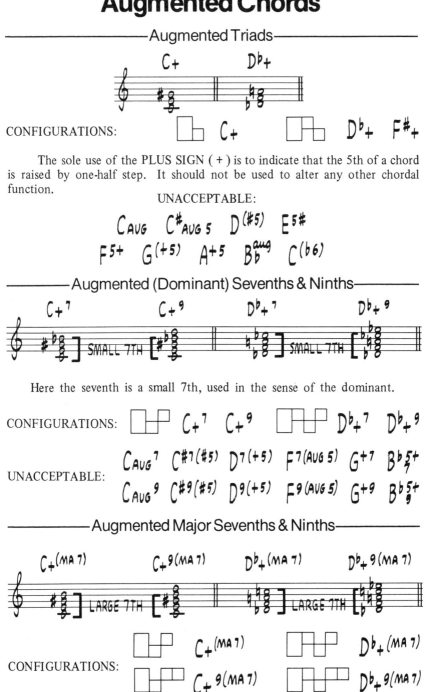

The previous examples can also be written as COMPOUND CHORDS (see page 36):

$C+^{(MA\ 7)} = E/C$

$C+^{9(MA\ 7)} = E^7/C$

$D\flat+^{(MA\ 7)} = F/D\flat$

$D\flat+^{9(MA\ 7)} = F^7/D\flat$

UNACCEPTABLE:

$C+^{(\sharp 7)}$ $D+^{7\sharp}$ $E\flat+^{7}$ $F_{AUG}+^{7}$ $G+^{(+7)}$ $A\flat+^{7+}$

$C+^{9(\sharp 7)}$ $D+^{9(7\sharp)}$ $E\flat+^{9}_{7}$ F_{AUG}^{9+7} $G+^{9(+7)}$ $A\flat+^{9(+7)}$

——————Augmented Minor Triads & Minor Sevenths——————

These chord alterations are ambiguous and should not be used. Enharmonically, the following occurs:

$C_{MI}+$ BECOMES $A\flat/C$

$C_{MI}+^{7}$ BECOMES $A\flat^{(ADD\ 9)}/C$

The transformations to A-FLAT and A-FLAT (ADD 9) are in the first inversion, having C as their lowest notes. This fact should be considered, and the symbols written as COMPOUND CHORDS (see page 36).

Chapter 8
Suspensions

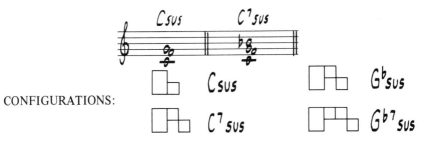

CONFIGURATIONS:

Academically, a suspension in a chord is a previous note held over, thereby delaying a resolution the ear expects to hear. Thus, in the academic sense, any note can become a suspension.

In the contemporary system of chord symbol writing, a suspension is not often used in the sense outlined above, but is more likely to be thought of as a self-contained identity that satisfies the ear, requiring no resolution. On that basis, the term "C MINOR SUSPENSION" is meaningless and should be discarded.

Employment of a COMPOUND CHORD symbol (see page 36) often eliminates ambiguity. For example, the expression "G 9TH SUSPENSION" might be shown as F6TH WITH A G BASS, or a D MINOR 7TH WITH A G BASS. Which of the latter to use might be influenced by the sequence of chords in the particular progression. Since the COMPOUND CHORD symbol is merely a device of convenience, the choice is an arbitrary one:

To some, the symbol for G 11TH is synonymous with that for G 9TH SUSPENSION, using the premise that in the G 11TH the 3rd of the chord is considered to be omitted (see DOMINANT ELEVENTHS, page 16). It is felt here that the G 9TH SUSPENSION is preferable inasmuch as the disposition of the 3rd is not left to chance; it <u>is</u> suspended, being replaced by the 4th degree above the root.

The same can be said for the 13TH CHORD containing a suspension; the COMPOUND CHORD substitutions for a G 13TH SUSPENSION are F MAJOR 7TH WITH A G BASS or D MINOR 9TH WITH A G BASS. Choice of alternates would depend, of course, upon whether or not the 5th ("D") is desired along with the 11th ("E").

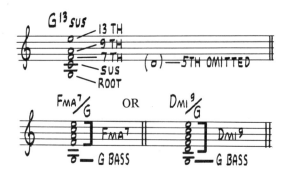

Higher-functioned "WHITE-NOTE CHORDS" are often miscalled SUSPENSIONS. In the following example the treble clef harmony remains the same over the bar line as only the bass changes. This does not mean a SUSPENSION, but instead two separate chords whose identities are determined by their bass notes. Obviously, not enough emphasis can be laid on naming the root of the structure.

(Examples of SUSPENSIONS WITH FLATTED NINTHS are shown in Chapter 10, COMPOUND CHORDS).

UNACCEPTABLE: $G^{SUS\,4}$ $A^{(ADD\,D)}$ $B\flat 7^{(ALT\,4)}$ $E7^{(+4)}$ $F7^{(\sharp 3)}$
$A\flat_{SUS}\,7$ $B7^{(SUS)}$ $G_{SUS}\,9$ $G\flat 9^{(SUS\,4)}$ $B\flat 9^{(E\flat)}$ $C4$

———————————— Suspended Diminished Sevenths ————————————

The SUSPENDED DIMINISHED CHORD shown above is sometimes given the symbol "C° (B TOP)", or "C° (ADD B)", both of which imply that the resolution, "A", is present along with the suspension. The chord is thereby muddied, losing its character in the process.

(The chord above can also be described as a COMPOUND CHORD, "B/C". See Chapter 10.)

Chapter 9
Chords with Altered Functions
—————————Flat Fifths—————————

The term "FLAT FIVE" best describes a chord containing the flat fifth. A MINUS SIGN (−) should not be used in this, or any, chord symbol to indicate the alteration of any function. In hasty, careless writing the minus sign is too easily overlooked or buried. Use the FLAT to mean a lowered chord element; substituting +4, ♯4 or AUG 4 for a FLAT FIFTH is meaningless.

(Note that in the following examples, altered functions are enclosed in parentheses.)

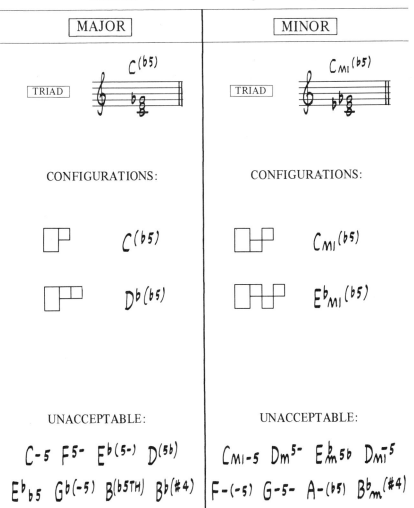

Flat Fifths (cont.)

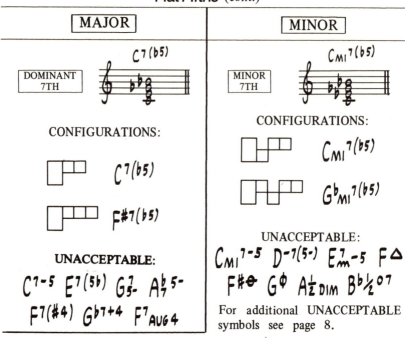

(The MINOR SEVENTH CHORD WITH A FLAT FIFTH is often referred to as the HALF-DIMINISHED CHORD. The triangle and other devices are frequently used to identify it. As the triangle is also in use to indicate a MAJOR SEVENTH CHORD, it is best that all such signs be discarded, thus eliminating ambiguities.)

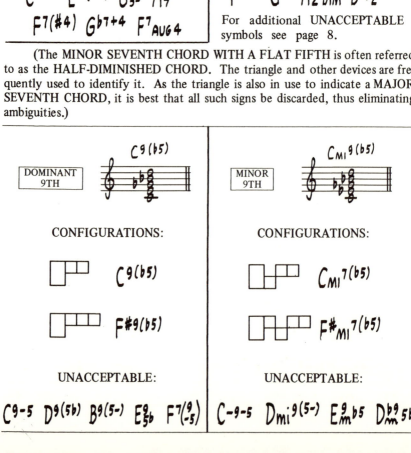

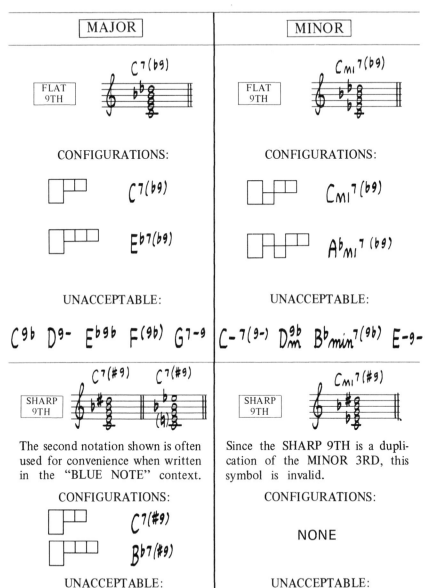

Altered Fifths & Ninths Combined

In multi-function chords, the highest function is placed at the top of the parentheses. This follows from the fact that chords are built in thirds from the lowest note to the highest. Again, when the 9th is altered, always include the 7th in the symbol.

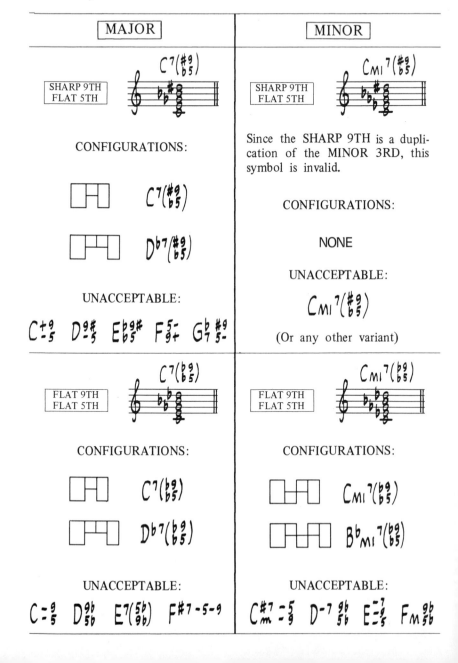

MAJOR	MINOR
 FLAT 9TH AUGMENTED 5TH	 FLAT 9TH AUGMENTED 5TH
CONFIGURATIONS: 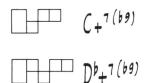	Best written out, but can be E-FLAT 7TH SUSPENSION WITH A C BASS. CONFIGURATIONS: NONE
UNACCEPTABLE: 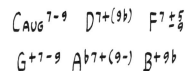	UNACCEPTABLE: (Or any other variant)
 SHARP 9TH AUGMENTED 5TH	 SHARP 9TH AUGMENTED 5TH
CONFIGURATIONS: 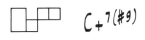	Since the SHARP 9TH is a duplication of the MINOR 3RD, this symbol is invalid. CONFIGURATIONS. NONE
UNACCEPTABLE: $C_{AUG}^{7}9\#$ $D^{7+(\#9)}$ $E^{7(^{+5}_{+9})}$ $F^{+9\#}$ $A\flat^{7}\binom{5\#}{9\#}$ B^{7+9+}	UNACCEPTABLE: $C_{MI+}^{7(\#9)}$ (Or any other variant)

Altered Elevenths

MAJOR	MINOR

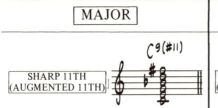 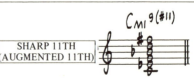

SHARP 11TH (AUGMENTED 11TH) — $C^{9(\sharp 11)}$

SHARP 11TH (AUGMENTED 11TH) — $C_{MI}^{9(\sharp 11)}$

In deference to historical use, the term "AUGMENTED 11TH" is included here. Do not interpret this to mean that the 5th is augmented.

CONFIGURATIONS:

$C^{9(\sharp 11)}$

$G^{\flat 9(\sharp 11)}$

CONFIGURATIONS:

$C_{MI}^{9(\sharp 11)}$

$E^{\flat}_{MI}{}^{9(\sharp 11)}$

UNACCEPTABLE:

C^{11+} $D^{11\sharp}$ $E^{(\sharp 11)}$ $F^{9(11\sharp)}$
$G^{7\binom{9}{\sharp 11}}$ $A^{\flat 7\binom{11\sharp}{+9}}$ $B^{\flat 9(\flat 12)}$ B^{9+11}

UNACCEPTABLE:

$Cm^{7\binom{+11}{+9}}$ $D_{MI}^{9(11+)}$ $E_{m}^{9}{}^{+11}$
Fmi^{+11} $G_{m}^{9\binom{\flat 5}{+5}}$ $A_{MI}^{9(11\sharp)}$

SHARP 11TH FLAT 9TH — $C^{7\binom{\sharp 11}{\flat 9}}$

SHARP 11TH FLAT 9TH — $C_{MI}^{7\binom{\sharp 11}{\flat 9}}$

CONFIGURATIONS:

$C^{7\binom{\sharp 11}{\flat 9}}$

$G^{\flat 7\binom{\sharp 11}{\flat 9}}$

CONFIGURATIONS:

$C_{MI}^{7\binom{\sharp 11}{\flat 9}}$

$F^{\sharp}_{MI}{}^{7\binom{\sharp 11}{\flat 9}}$

UNACCEPTABLE:

$C^{7}{}^{9-}_{11+}$ $D^{7}{}^{\sharp 9}_{+11}$ $E^{\flat 11+(\flat 9)}$ $F^{+11}_{9\flat}$

UNACCEPTABLE:

$Cm^{7(-9)}_{(+11)}$ $D^{\flat}_{m}{}^{7}{}^{9\flat}_{11+}$ $Emi^{7}{}^{9-}_{11\sharp}$ $F^{-7}{}^{\binom{9-}{+11}}$

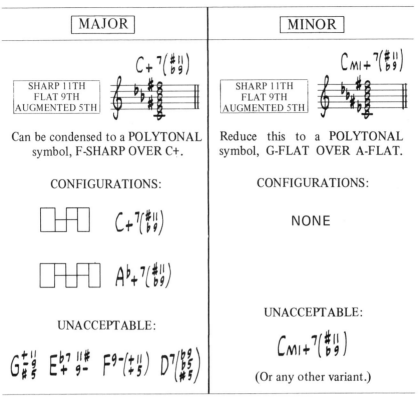

The later examples clearly show that eventually the process becomes self-defeating, musical shorthand ceases to exist, and the goal of INSTANT CHORD RECOGNITION AND ANALYSIS is never reached. While the possible number of chromatically altered chordal functions is finite, in the practical sense it is unreasonable to ask the player to have all of these combinations stored away for instant read-out.

AS ADVOCATED THROUGHOUT THESE PAGES, THE MORE COMPLEX ALTERED CHORDS SHOULD BE WRITTEN OUT IN PROPER NOTATION, ALWAYS INCLUDING THE BASS NOTE TO INDICATE THE INVERSION.

It is beyond the purview of this book to include examples of every possible altered chord. Suffice it to say that the practice of regarding the chord structure as a stacking up of thirds is the key to accurate analysis. Each note is thereby given its proper title and can be altered up or down one-half step as the writer desires.

Certainly the simplest and most concise chord symbol is the best one, as long as it conveys the desired information; the use of COMPOUND and POLYTONAL symbols can often reduce the most highly altered five and six-part chords to a more comprehensive form. These are treated in the following chapters.

Chapter 10
Compound Chords

The COMPOUND CHORD symbol is most useful to describe highly altered chords. By definition, the symbol to the left of the diagonal slash line designates a chord; the letter to the right of the slash indicates a single note, the bass.

CONFIGURATION: ◰   E7/C   Db7/Gb

(Referred to as: "E-SEVENTH WITH A C BASS" and
"D-FLAT SEVENTH WITH A G-FLAT BASS")

No pretense is made that the COMPOUND CHORD has academic validity. For example, in the expression, "E-SEVENTH WITH A C BASS", the symbol E7 has no standing as the dominant 7th of the key of A. In this case, E7 merely means that the chord consists of an E, G-sharp, B and D, reading upward. The bass note, C, is not necessarily related to the key of F in the dominant sense, so "E7TH WITH A C BASS" is its own being.

| EXAMPLES |

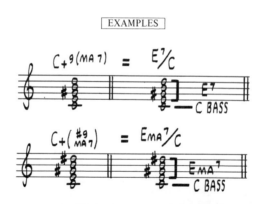

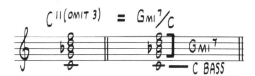

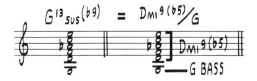

The preceding examples, chords chosen at random, should serve to outline the method of converting complex chords to COMPOUND CHORDS by using simple harmonic analysis. It is apparent that at times these complexities are irreducible; in such cases the chord should be written out.

Use of the COMPOUND CHORD symbol need not be confined to five-and six-part structures. It may also be used for triads, inversions and pedal points:

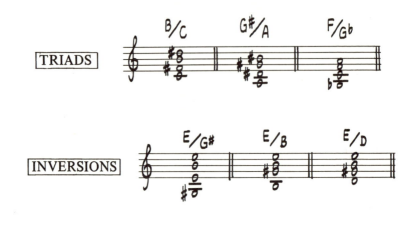

Referring to the first chord example at the top of the page (B/C), and translating it into a more conventional symbol, B/C becomes a C MINOR WITH A MAJOR 7TH AND A FLAT 5TH, which at first glance is not readily recognizable for what it is, a B MAJOR TRIAD WITH A C BASS:

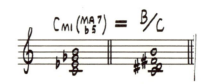

This again illustrates the serviceability of the COMPOUND CHORD symbol.

UNACCEPTABLE:

G/B Bass   A♭(E♭ Bass)   D♭ A♭ Bs

Chapter 11

Polytonal Chords

This familiar six-part POLYTONAL CHORD achieved recognition as the so-called "PETROUCHKA CHORD" of Stravinsky.

CONFIGURATION:

□ $\dfrac{F\#}{C}$

Note that the symbol uses a horizontal line to separate its elements and is referred to (using the above) as "F-SHARP OVER C", meaning there are two chord structures, one above the other.

A POLYTONAL symbol can in many cases serve to clarify the identity of complex, highly altered six-and seven-part chords. (Again, as with COMPOUND CHORDS, we cite the academic disclaimer and repeat that irreducible complexities should be written out.)

EXAMPLES

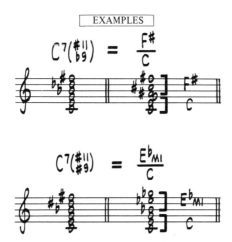

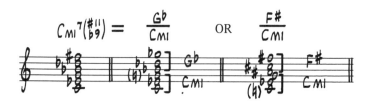

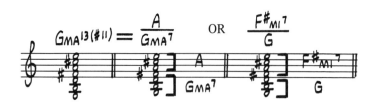

The foregoing examples demonstrate the greater readability of the POLYTONAL symbol compared to a highly altered chord symbol. The same principles of harmonic analysis hold here as set forth earlier, especially in the chapter on COMPOUND CHORDS.

Chapter 12
Miscellany

──────── Fourth Chords ────────

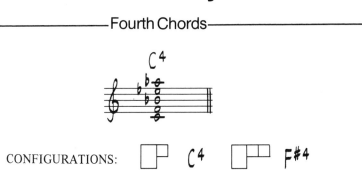

FOURTH CHORDS consist of perfect 4ths stacked on each other. The practical limit is five voices, after which dissonance presents itself.

Analysis by thirds shows that the five-note example of C4 shown above is merely an expanded inversion of an A-FLAT 6/9 CHORD WITH A C BASS.

These structures are only of passing interest and should be fully written out with the actual notes to clearly indicate the context, which generally is a maximum of four voices, especially for guitar.

By and large, a shorthand symbol for the FOURTH CHORD tells us very little and is impractical.

──────── Omitted Notes ────────

For greatest clarity, chords with omitted notes are best written out.

CONFIGURATIONS:

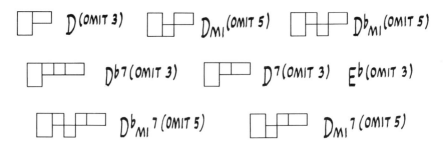

(The expression "OMIT" is preferable to "NO".)

"OMIT" can be continued through 7ths and 9ths. However, a 9TH CHORD that omits the 3rd is better shown as a COMPOUND CHORD.

Concerning Registers

When writing rhythm parts, consideration should be given to the whole musical picture. Who is playing what, and in which register? Is there a sustained background and if so, will the higher-order altered functions clash with it and muddy the texture? A catch-all omnibus rhythm part that is meant to serve everyone from the bass on up through the keyboards is not always the answer. Discretion should be used, for there are many times when sections of an arrangement or composition would benefit if separate parts were written for bass, guitar(s) and keyboard(s). This is particularly true when dealing with amplified and electronic instruments, whose tendency to generate overtones, many of them spurious, can be a distinct disadvantage.

The following will serve to illustrate:

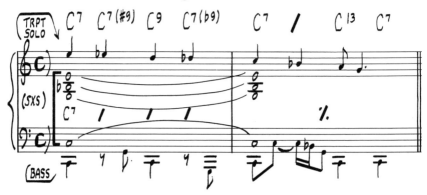

If, in the example above, the mid-range rhythm instruments played every chord change indicated, an octave doubling of the solo trumpet occurs. A much cleaner sound is achieved if the rhythm were to play C7 straight through the two measures, letting the trumpet create the higher functions.

In the next example, a futile use of complex symbols has been made in attempting to indicate every note present. Rhythm instruments playing the highly altered functions in their normal mid-range, would create congestion against the sustaining trombones, which are playing a pure C CHORD. In this situation, it is patently desirable that the middle instruments also play pure C CHORDS.

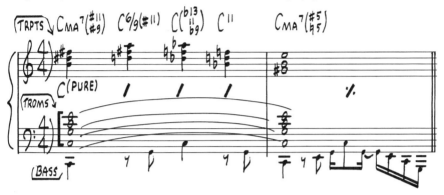

Even if there were no sustaining trombones in the above example, it would still be desirable to restrict the mid-range rhythm instruments to a pure C CHORD. Thus, the basic harmony would be firmly established beneath the triadic superstructures. In the event the composer desired to communicate the full harmonic content of the chords with a single notation, a much clearer concept can be obtained by converting the complex symbols to POLYTONAL symbols, as follows:

$$C_{MA}7(\sharp_{\sharp 9}^{\sharp 11}) = \frac{B}{C}$$

$$C6/9(\sharp 11) = \frac{D}{C}$$

$$C\binom{\flat 13}{11}_{\flat 9} = \frac{D\flat}{C}$$

$$C^{11} = \frac{B\flat}{C}$$

$$C_{MA}7(\sharp_{\natural 5}^{\sharp 5}) = \frac{E}{C}$$

However, when all-inclusive chord symbols are given, judicious and tasteful placement of notes by the players is mandatory. The possibility of octave doubling would be present, which would nullify the clearly polytonal effect the composer desired. To dispel any doubt, be explicit as to what each mid-range instrument is to do. In cases like the one above, an all-inclusive symbol (POLYTONAL or not), can be guilty of supplying <u>too</u> much information.

THE BEST CHORD SYMBOL IS THE SIMPLEST ONE.

Chapter 13

In Summation

It is hoped that this volume will aid in establishing a uniform system of standard chord symbols, clearly written and easily understood by musicians of all skills.

To reach these ends, the following steps should be kept in mind:

1. Analyze chords on a rational basis, referring to Chapter 2, "THE RAW MATERIAL OF CHORDS".

2. Employ the signs and symbols given in Chapter 3, "BASIC RULES".

3. Eliminate the exotic signs that have dual or uncertain meanings.

4. Where possible, simplify highly altered chords by converting them to COMPOUND or POLYTONAL SYMBOLS.

5. When the symbol becomes too complex or top-heavy, write out the chords in notation.

6. Use the configurations shown. Understand their principle.

As much care must be given to writing a rhythm part as to any other; rhythm parts are not mere after-thoughts. In a free electric bass part using chord symbols, it is nonsensical to include all of the altered 9ths, 11ths and 13ths that might occur in the guitar or keyboard parts. Simplify, indicating only the substance of the chord in the symbol.

Be consistent. Learn the simple, basic rules and uniform practices contained here and observe them. The writer is thereby justified in insisting that his chord symbols be copied verbatim, without benefit of injudicious editing performed by an unqualified person. This is especially true when a score is divided and worked on by more than one copyist at the same time. Under these circumstances, the results can be quite ragged; rarely are disparate editorial opinions alike.

A uniform and standard system is of value in organizing and clarifying the task of placing chord symbols on paper. It would be rewarding to believe that an even greater benefit might be derived from these concepts. It is:

BEFORE WRITING ... THINK.

About the Authors

Carl Brandt has participated in the gamut of the musical experience: Pop, Rock, Jazz, Symphonic, Concert Band, Phonograph Recordings, Live TV, Motion Pictures and TV Film. These activities are as composer, conductor, arranger, orchestrator, instrumentalist and publisher. Staff positions include engagements at Warner Brothers, Disney Studios and EDJ Music. Mr. Brandt is currently involved in free-lance work for motion pictures and television.

Clinton Roemer has long been one of the most prominent music copyists on the Hollywood scene, working in all fields of the entertainment industry. While operating his own music preparation service, Mr. Roemer collaborated with many composer/arrangers, as well as acting as exclusive copyist for a number of recording artists. He is also author of the best-selling text, THE ART OF MUSIC COPYING, the most widely accepted and comprehensive treatment on the craft of preparing music for performance.

ALSO PUBLISHED BY ROERICK MUSIC CO.

A MUST FOR ALL MUSIC EDUCATORS, STUDENTS AND LIBRARIES

The Art of Music Copying

THE PREPARATION OF MUSIC FOR PERFORMANCE
SECOND EDITION (1985)

by Clinton Roemer

Contents

CHAPTER		
	1	GLOSSARY
	2	EQUIPMENT, MATERIAL AND SUPPLIES
	3	BEGINNING TO WRITE
	4	RESTS AND MULTIPLE BAR RESTS
	5	NOTES, FLAGS AND LEDGER LINES
	6	CLEFS, ACCIDENTALS, SIGNS, SYMBOLS AND ABBREVIATIONS
	7	SPACING
	8	BEAMS
	9	KEY SIGNATURES AND TIME SIGNATURES
	10	SLURS AND TIES
	11	PHRASING
	12	CHORDS
	13	NOTATION
	14	ENGLISH ON PARTS
	15	EDITING
	16	RANGE AND TRANSPOSITION CHARTS
	17	TRANSPOSITION
	18	PREPARING A SCORE AND PARTS FOR COPYING
	19	COPYING AN ORCHESTRA PART
	20	DRUM AND PERCUSSION PARTS
	21	GUITAR PARTS
	22	KEYBOARD PARTS
	23	HARP PARTS
	24	STRING PARTS
	25	MASTER LAYOUT PARTS
	26	VOCAL PARTS, LEAD SHEETS AND SONG COPIES
	27	CHOIR PARTS
	28	CONDUCTOR PARTS.
	29	MISCELLANEOUS
	30	CLOSING

Size — 8¾" x 12"
216 pages
Approx. 1000 examples

— Free descriptive brochure on request —

ROERICK MUSIC CO.
4046 Davana Road
Sherman Oaks, Calif. 91423